The 30 Day NICU Devotional

"Taking each day & each moment, one step at a time."

The 30 Day

NICU

Devotional

"Taking each day & each moment, one step at a time."

Author: Mariann W. Shaw

Contributing Editor: Nancymarie Bassett

Published By: Shaw's Publishing Inc. © 2017

First Printing: 2017

ISBN 9781365790447

Shaw's Publishing Inc.
PO BOX 292172
Lewisville, TX 75029

www.masgnicu.org

Ordering Information:

Special discounts are available on quantity purchases by corporations, associations, educators, and others. For details, contact the Publisher at the above listed address.

U.S. trade bookstores and wholesalers: Please contact Mariann Shaw for Shaw's Publishing Tel: (972) 603-5165 or email mariann@masgnicu.org

I dedicate this devotional to my son, Maison Alexander Jerkins ~ Shaw (My Mojo). I thank God for you and I love you so much! You showed me who I was and who I needed to become in order to be the Mother God wanted me to be for you. Within our neonatal journey, you taught me how to fight. You taught me how to pray. And you taught me how to really trust God. I'm so happy and proud to not only be a NICU Parent and Survivor; but I'm blessed, humbled and grateful to be your mother.

I will always and forever love you!

"Mommy" ~ Marian W. Shaw

TABLE OF CONTENTS

Preface..7
Introduction "What Did I do Wrong?"...................8
Encouraging Scriptures on Hope.........................18
Give It to God (Prayer).....................................31
Encouraging Scriptures to Keep in Mind..................35
Encouraging Scriptures on Faith..........................47
Give It to God (Prayer).....................................59
Your Reflection "Let's Take a Look".....................61
Encouraging Scriptures on Prayer.........................67
Give It to God(Prayer)......................................79
Inspiring Quotes for NICU................................85
Give It to God (Prayer).....................................97
Encouraging Scriptures on Peace.........................102
Different Prayers for Different Subjects.................124
The NICU Buddy Program...................................126
A Note from the Author....................................134
Additional Journal Entries.................................136

PREFACE

The 30 Day NICU Devotional

The 30 Day NICU Devotional is a month's worth of encouragements from the neonatal experience. The devotions are quick and inspiring, and fit for the busy NICU schedule. From scriptures to prayers, small journal exercises and powerful uplifting quotes, it's all intended as a supplement to your daily living with encouragement on building and maintaining a relationship with God. While the neonatal life can drain families with the ups and downs along the way, this devotional will encourage, inspire and re-strengthen.

This Devotional was written with intent for NICU families; however open to all. If you are outside the NICU community and wish to restart the next 30 days with positive reinforcements, encouragements, scriptures and prayers – this devotional is for you as well.

WHAT DID I DO WRONG?

(Introduction)

I was 26 weeks pregnant thinking, "Everything is fine. The doctor is going to come back in the room and tell me that my blood pressure was high but now everything is stable and I can go home." I laid there with my eyes closed picturing a calm beach with beautiful waves and total serenity. Unfortunately, in reality nothing was calm. Instead there was nothing but fear. Before I knew it, I was admitted into the hospital and was assigned to strict bed rest. My blood pressure was 195/90 and I was immediately diagnosed with Preeclampsia. Nothing was improving, in fact, two weeks passed and everything was getting worse. My son's heart rate was dropping and I was getting closer and closer to chances of seizers and all sorts of things. At 28 weeks, my son came into the world only weighing 2pds and 10oz; once the water weight dropped he was officially 1pd and 10oz.

My heart ached because my son was too tiny for me to hold him. He could only hold my pinky-finger and he could only do it in silence. I remember thinking, "What did I do wrong? What should I have done differently to avoid such an overbearing struggle?"

In the Bible there are numerous stories where I find myself asking "I wonder *why that* happened?" An example I don't mind using is Moses's mother. Instead of putting her baby in basket and allowing him to move down stream, why didn't she run away and flee the City? She didn't have family at all? Was there not *anyone else* that could help her? Then I started to think about her son's destiny and his outcome. If baby Moses wasn't placed in a basket, who would have lead the people out of Israel? Who would have discovered God face to face through those different level of plagues and trails? So instead of looking at the glass half empty, I begin to look at the glass half full. I started to Google search different organizations that specialize in Preeclampsia, prematurity, pregnancy stress and single mothers in the neonatal; I couldn't help but to think "How can I use our story to help others?"

For Moses, everything happened for a reason to help get him to where he was supposed to be. Perhaps for Maison and I everything happened for a reason to help get us to where we need to be.

How does that reflect on your situation in particular?

The Bible encourages us that all things work together for the good of them who love the Lord and that are called to his purpose. God gave me a revelation and showed me that if I continue to dwell in the past then I will never be able to get to the good part. I believe that with our trials and tribulations there are lessons within them and if we dwell on the bad we will never get to the other side of where we are supposed to be; the victory side.

You have a purpose in this life. Your neonatal journey will help someone that is in the same situation as you. You are here for a reason and the same applies to your fighting baby. Life decided to give you a road that requires a different level of parenting, patience's, perseverance, hope, faith, trust in God and a stronger prayer life. Use this journey to have a deeper connection with God, yourself, and your family to push forward.

Everything will be ok and please know **you didn't do anything wrong**...

Mariann <3

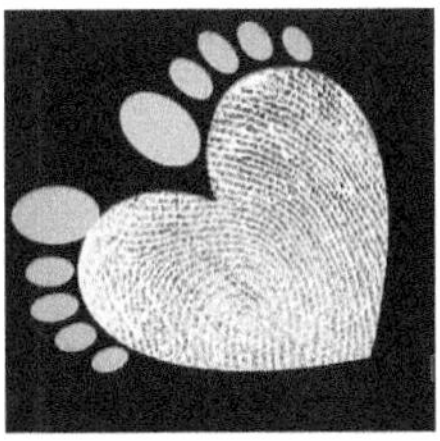

Let us then approach God's throne of grace with confidence, so that we may receive mercy and find grace to help us in our time of need.

Hebrew 4:16

EACH DAY ONE STEP AT A TIME...

Encouragement – Day 1

Matthew 6:34

"Therefore do not worry about tomorrow, for tomorrow will worry about itself. Each day has enough trouble of its own."

There is no law or rule and that says, "Today you must do it all. Today you must master it all. Today you must and you shall complete all tasks, trials and tribulations given to you. Do it all and get it all done today!" It's humanly impossible and simply unfair. It's unfair to you to allow that kind of demand emotionally, spiritually and physically.

Set three simple goals and take your time working towards them for this entire week. If you only finish one out of three, you still did an awesome job! Being a mother/father of a little one that is fighting and growing in the NICU is no easy task. There's breast pumping around the clock, NICU visits, paperwork, questions for the specialist and emotions that are constantly running up and down. Not to leave out life in general still taking place outside the NICU. That's a lot by itself!

Be encourage and handle this day with the grace that was given to you. Yesterday might have been hard, but guess what, you made it through and today is a new day! Be positive, smile and give all of your cares and worries to God.

1 Peter 5:7

"Cast all your anxiety on him because he cares for you."

Today: Pray for direction, peace & joy.

I REMEMBER WHEN…

My Reflection, Your Encouragement – Day 2

It was a Saturday afternoon and I had just returned back to the NICU from taking my godmother to the airport. I was watching my son sleep in his incubator when suddenly it hit me. I was alone. I remember thinking, "When I leave here and go home, it's going to be me, just me, by myself in my home. And when I come back here tomorrow, it's going to be just me and my son." I placed my hand on my son's incubator and said "Babe, it's just us. Everyone went home. We're going to get through this together." Tears fell from my eyes and I silently cried by my son's bedside.

Within that moment, I could feel someone standing behind me. I whipped my face, turned around, and saw no one was there. But still, I could *feel* someone standing behind me. He suddenly spoke to me and said "You know that's not true. I'm here with you and your son, *always*; and no matter what happens, you will never be alone." God's voice was still, firm, sweet and peaceful. "I will never leave you or forsake you. NEVER." I felt His presents and His peace come over me and settle my spirit. It settled the moment and my heart. When I finally calmed down, I explained to God that I knew I wasn't completely alone, but within that moment, it just felt like it.

I had a human moment. I had an honest moment. Even today, you might have a moment of feeling alone, defeated or helpless. It's ok. Have your moment, but keep going! Keep pressing through the journey; and while you press through, please know, in fact, that you are ***not*** alone. God is with you! He will never leave you or forsake you. He will always and forever be with you.

Hebrew 13:5

"Never will I leave you; never will I forsake you."

Today: Pray for strength, comfort & healing.

HOPE

Scriptures on Hope – Day 3

I encourage you to hope *for*:

- Life
- Great Health
- Strength
- Peace
- Healing
- Restoration
- Faith
- Love
- Joy
- Strength

…and continue to add to the list.

Today: Pray for the strength of hope.

ENCOURAGING SCRIPTURES

Hope – Day 4

Jeremiah 29:11 "For I know the thoughts that I think toward you, says the LORD, thoughts of peace and not of evil, to give you a future and a hope."

Psalms 45:11 Why, my soul, are you downcast? Why so disturbed within me? Put your hope in God, for I will yet praise him, my Savior and my God.

Isaiah 40:31 But those who hope in the Lord will renew their strength. They will soar on wings like eagles; they will run and not grow weary, they will walk and not be faint.

Romans 15:13 May the God of hope fill you with all joy and peace as you trust in him, so that you may overflow with hope by the power of the Holy Spirit.

Palms 121:7-8 The Lord will keep you from all harm, he will watch over your life; the Lord will watch over your coming and going both now and forevermore.

Romans 15:13 May the God of hope fill you with all joy and peace as you trust in him, so that you may overflow with hope by the power of the Holy Spirit.

Psalms 31:24 Be strong and take heart, all you who hope in the Lord.

1 Corinthians 15:19 If in Christ we have hope in this life only, we are of all people most to be pitied.

Romans 12:12 Rejoice in hope, be patient in tribulation, be constant in prayer.

Joshua 10:25 Joshua said to them, "Do not be afraid; do not be discouraged. Be strong and courageous.

Job 6:8 Oh that I might have my request, that God would grant what I hope for.

Psalm 147:11 The Lord delights in those who fear Him, who put their hope in his unfailing love.

Hebrews 10:23 Let us hold unswervingly to the hope we profess, for He who promised is faithful.

Psalms 130:5 I wait for the Lord, my whole being waits, and in His word I put my hope.

Micah 7:7 But as for me, I watch in hope for the Lord, I wait for God my Savior; my God will hear me.

Lamentations 3:24 I say to myself, "The Lord is my portion; therefore, I will wait for Him."

Psalm 33:22 May your unfailing love be with us, Lord, even as we put our hope in you.

1 Peter 1:3 Praise be to the God and Father of our lord Jesus Christ! In His great mercy he has given us new birth into a

living hope through the resurrection of Jesus Christ from the dead.

Ephesians 4:4 There is one body and one Spirit, just as you were called to one hope when you were called.

Today: Pray for faith, peace & rest.

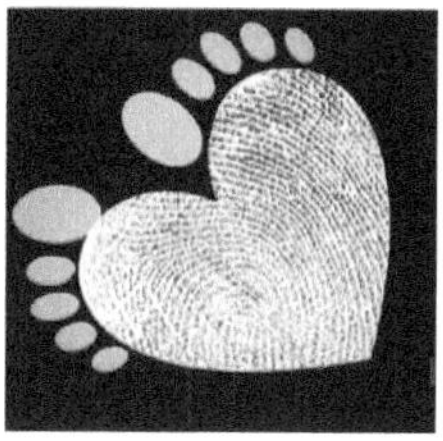

But those who trust in the Lord will find new strength.

They will soar high on wings like eagles.

They will run and not grow weary.

They will walk and not faint.

Isaiah 40:31

TODAY I FEEL…

Your reflection – Day 5

Complete your journal entry. List all of your emotions, things that are taking place in the NICU, and your prayers.

Date: __/__/____

Today: Pray for healing.

GIVE IT TO GOD

Yesterday's Entry, Today's Prayer – Day 6

Yesterday you wrote a journal entry. Today, we're going to pray together concerning all the things you listed.

Read this prayer out loud:

Dear Heavenly Father,

First and foremost: Thank you. Thank you for allowing me to see this day. Thank you for the new mercies, grace and favor that you have given me this day. Thank you for keeping me and my family. Thank you for your traveling grace to my home and the NICU every day. Thank you for being my friend and always being here with and for me. Thank you! I don't take you, life and this moment for granted. Before I ask of thing, I just want to say thank you.

Heavenly Father, please forgive me. Forgive me of my sins that I have committed and the sins I didn't realize I have committed. I apologize and ask that you forgive me. Please create in me a clean heart and renew the right spirit within me.

Father, you see everything I have written out. You even see things I didn't write out and choose to keep close to my heart. Everything concerning my baby, the NICU, our home, my stress, worries, doubts, fears and concerns. I have placed as much as I could on here in my devotional and journal. I know and believe that you see it all. You see beyond what's listed here, you see my heart. You see my baby in the NICU. You see my home. You see my family.

You see it all! Father God, I give all of this to you. In faith, I give you my stress and worries and I believe you will take care of it all. You said in your word to cast all of my anxiety on you because you care for me. I believe your word and I trust you.

Father God, I am doing my absolute best, but I cannot do this without you. I need you not only in my situations but also in my life. In my baby's life, my family's life, in our home and in our hearts. I rebuke Satan and evil spiritual wickedness. No weapon formed against my baby and our home shall prosper. I believe you will heal, deliver and rescue my baby in the NICU as well as our entire family. In Jesus's name I pray, Amen.

If you wish to pray and talk to God more, feel free to do so. Continue to cast all of your cares upon God. He loves you, He cares for you and He will always and forever be with you. *If you would like to give your life to Christ, please turn to the* ***Repentance Prayer*** *along with additional prayers.* *(page 124).*

HAVE I ASKED A QUESTION TODAY?

The NICU – Day 7

"There's no such thing as a stupid question." ~ Anonymous

Proverbs 4:7

"Wisdom is the principle thing; therefore, get wisdom; and with all thy getting get understanding."

During my NICU journey I made an effort to ask questions. Whatever I was doing, if a question popped into my mine, I made note of it and took it with met to the NICU. I asked the nurses, doctors and specialist. At one point I joked, "you know I'm the question lady, so I have to ask!"

Make it a habit to ask questions. The statement is true: **knowledge is power!** The more you know, the more you understand; so when it's time to bring the baby home, it will help you be more at ease. Read up on things and then ask questions about what you just read. Please keep in mind: you can't always trust things on the internet. So I would suggest to ask the specialist and or the doctor if there is anything in particular that they want you to read; and if so, read it during your down time. Don't make it a stressful step, let it be educational, helpful and relaxing.

Your questions:

Today: Pray for laughter, joy & balance.

ENCOURAGING SCRIPTURES

Keep in Mind – Day 8

Philippians 4:6-7 Be careful for noting; but in everything by prayer and supplication with thanksgiving let your requests be made known unto God. And the peace of God, which passes all understanding, shall keep your hearts and minds through Christ Jesus.

Psalm 46:1-3 God is our refuge and strength, a very present help in trouble. Therefore will not we fear, though the earth be removed, and though the mountains be carried into the midst of the sea.

Psalm 138:7 Though I walk in the midst of trouble, thou wilt revive me: thou shalt stretch forth thine hand against the wreath of mine enemies, and thy right hand shall save me.

Matthew 11:28 Come unto me, all ye that labor and are heavy burden, and I will give you rest.

Psalm 55:22 Cast all thy burden upon the Lord, and he shall sustain thee: he shall never suffer the righteous to be moved.

Psalm 27:14 Wait on the Lord: be of good courage, and he shall strengthen thine heart: wait, I say, on the Lord.

Psalms 31:24 Be of good courage, and he shall strengthen your heart, all ye that hope in the Lord.

Philippians 4:12-13 I can do all things through Christ which strengthens me.

Hebrews 11:1 Now faith is the substances of things hoped for, the evidence of things not seen.

James 1:5-6 If any of you lack wisdom, let him ask of God, that giveth to all men liberally, and upbraideth not; and it shall be given him. But let him ask in faith, nothing wavering. For he that wavereth is like a wave of the sea driven with the wind and tossed.

Psalms 71:5 For thou art my hope, Oh Lord God: though art my trust from my youth.

2 Thessalonians 3:16 Now the Lord of peace himself give you peace always by all means.

John 14:27 Peace I leave with you, my peace I give unto you: not as the world giveth, give I unto you. Let not your heart be troubled, neither let it be afraid.

Proverbs 3:5-6 Trust in the Lord with all thine heart; and lean not unto thine own understanding. In all thy ways acknowledge Him and He shall direct your paths.

1 Peter 5:7 Casting all your care upon Him; for He cares for you.

Psalm 40:4 Blessed is that man that maketh the Lord his trust.

Philippians 4:19 But God shall supply all your needs according to the riches in glory by Christ Jesus.

Romans 8:28 And we know that all things work together for good to them that love God, to them who are called according to His purpose.

Psalms 23 The Lord is my shepherd, I lack nothing. He makes me lie down in green pastures, he leads me beside quiet waters, he refreshes my soul. He guides me along the right paths for his names' sake. Even though I walk through the darkest valley, I will fear no evil, for you are with me; your rod and your staff, they comfort me. You prepare a table before me in the presence of my enemies. You anoint my head with oil; my cup overflows. Surely your goodness and love will follow me all the days of my life, and I will dwell in the house of the Lord forever.

Ecclesiastes 3:1 There is a time for everything, and a season for every activity under the Heavens.

Everyone has a purpose in their life. Allow this NICU season to be used for something good. Share your journey with your NICU neighbor. Give encouraging, hopeful, and peaceful words. Sometimes encouraging others helps encourage ourselves.

Today: Pray for direction, protection & peace.

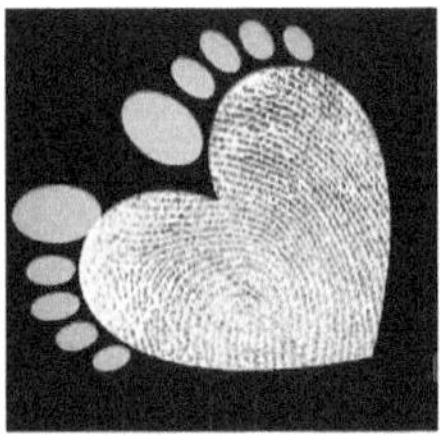

I seek you with all my heart…

Do not let me stray from your commands.

Psalm 119:10

SPEAK LIFE

Your Mind has Power – Day 9

Proverbs 23:7

"For as he thinketh in his heart, so is he."

Have you ever paid attention to your thoughts? Have you ever noticed that if you think and meditate on an issue, an event, or a problem that sooner or later your attitude reflects your behavior? Example: when I was finally discharged from the hospital, on my way home, I thought constantly about my baby in the NICU. I felt horrible because I felt as though I was leaving him at the hospital with no care; when in actuality, that was not true. But the devil wanted me to think about it that way. When I arrived home, my mother was in the kitchen cooking and had my place spotless. I was grateful but because I was thinking negatively, I started fussing about things I couldn't find instead of asking for them. The more I allowed my mind to wonder with negative thoughts, the more I fussed. If you wake up and think horrible thoughts and allow yourself to be overtaken by doom and gloom, it will eventually reflect in your overall attitude and behavior.

When you start your day, start it with prayer. Talk to God and tell Him what's on your heart and mind. Let Him know how you feel about the day before and ask Him to give you peace and strength for it. End your prayer with speaking positively into your day. Speak great things over your baby's life. Speak into your atmosphere. Think great and be great!

Finish this phrase by writing out positive outcomes.

Today, I will:

Be happy.
Laugh.
Smile.
Think only great things. (continue)

Today: Think on things that's positive & true.

YOUR SUPPORT SYSTEM MATTERS

What does your circle reflect? – Day 10

Yesterday, I encouraged you to speak into your atmosphere. Today, let's take a look your surroundings and support system: the people around you. Let's be real -- are they truly supportive? When someone comes around, are they brining negative comments and negative feedback? From your NICU situation to life in general, are they negative? You want everything and everyone to work together and along with the positivity you're striving for. It will be a struggle to speak positive and great things into your atmosphere and someone comes around with negative energy. All of your strength, energy and focus needs to be on your baby and the overall progress in the NICU. Wither your support system is family and or a group of friends, if someone is constantly giving you a push back and not being respectful, positive and encouraging; let them know in a polite way and move forward. Do this not just for your NICU journey but make this an ongoing tone for your life and home. We only live once! Refuse to live in turmoil, negative energy and unnecessary stress/drama.

Take Note:

- Is your circle actively supportive?
- Is your circle encouraging?
- Is your circle prayerful?
- Is your circle willing to help and make days easy?

- ❖ Is your circle constantly making you think on things you cannot control?
- ❖ Is your circle stressful?
- ❖ Is your circle negative?

Reevaluate, politely address, reset the tone and move forward.

Today: Pray for guidance, peace & joy.

FAITH IS KEY

Faith – Day 11

During my journey in the NICU, when it was time to go home for the night, I always heard, "Have faith and believe that when you're not here, everything will be alright."

The word encourages us that faith is the substances of things hoped for and the evidence of things not seen. We look at situations in our lives and pray and hope for particular outcomes. Some of us walk in hope with the idea of it already being done. That's awesome!

I would like to encourage you in your NICU journey to walk in your hope and faith knowing that at the end of the day, when it's time to go home for the night, to have faith and believe that when you're not there, everything will be alright. Furthermore, with each trail that is presented to you (a procedure, medicine, oxygen, test, diagnose, outcome predictions, etc.), have faith for a brighter and better outcome. Pray, have faith when you pray, trust God and believe!

Finish this phrase by writing out positive outcomes.

I encourage you to have faith in:

- Praying.
- Your NICU journey.
- Your request to God.

- ❖ Your life.
- ❖ In every situation. (Continue to add to the list.)

Today: Pray for increase of faith, strength & peace.

I REMEMBER WHEN…

My Reflection, Your Encouragement – Day 12

I can recall a time when my son was progressing really good and in response to that they allowed him to have "a busy" week. Being in the NICU, you (the reader) understand that too much stimulation for a premature baby can be overwhelming to him/her and cause a few minor setbacks. Maison was no longer on room air and was sleeping outside of his incubator. In addition, he received a shot that week and started eating from a bottle. Two days later, he nursed from me for the first time. I remember being so excited because it there was so much progress in one week and he was rocking it. The next day (after our first nursing session), I walked in and noticed my son was back on room air. I literally froze and just stood there. One of his nurses assured me that it was normal for a few setbacks when a lot is experienced for the first time. It was something small but felt major. I didn't offer to nurse, because I wanted him to get his rest. I wanted his strength back up so we could continue to move forward.

That night when I went home, I gave God an emotional prayer. I remember saying to God, "I just want him to continue to progress and move forward. I want my baby home." What I'm about to say might seem bazar, but I'm being honest about what I prayed for. I told God, "You specialize in miracles. You specialize in the impossible. God, please give my son strength so by the end of the week, he is no longer on room air. No more air from here on out."

Before that week was over, my son had his strength back and was off room air! This time it was for good!

Whenever you take your request to God in prayer, have faith and believe in your prayer. Don't go to God doubting, guessing, assuming the worse and thinking "this may not work." That's what the devil wants you to think and believe. The devil wants you to believe that your conversations to God doesn't matter. Well, I am writing you this to encourage you and let you know—YOUR PRAYERS MATTER! God hears you and most importantly, He loves you. When you pray, BELIEVE AND HAVE FAITH.

Today: Make today a faith believing day! Doubt of any kind is simply not welcomed! Pray for an increase in your faith.

ENCOURAGING SCRIPTURES

There's Power in Faith – Day 13

James 1:6 But let him ask in faith, nothing wavering. For he that wavers is like a wave of the sea driven with the wind and tossed.

Hebrews 11:1 Now faith is the substance of things hoped for, the evidence of things not seen.

1 Peter 1:21 Who by him do believe in God, that raised him up from the dead, and gave him glory; that your faith and hope might be in God.

Mark 11:24 Therefore, I say unto you, whatsoever things you desire, when you pray, believe that you receive them, and you shall have them.

Matthew 21:22 If you believe, you will receive, whatever you ask for in prayer

Hebrews 11:6 And without faith it is impossible to please Him, for he who comes to God must believe that He is and that He is a rewarder of those who seek Him.

Ephesians 3:12 In whom we have boldness and confident access through faith in Him.

Galatians 3:26 For ye are the children of God by faith in Christ Jesus.

Mark 11:22-23 And Jesus answering saith unto them, "Have faith in God. For verily I say unto you, that whosoever shall say unto this mountain, 'Be though removed, and be though cast into the sea;' and shall not doubt in his heart, but shall believe that those things which he saith shall come to pass, he shall have whatever he saith."

2 Corinthians 5:7 For we walk by faith, and not by sight.

Galatians 5:22-23 The fruit of the Spirit is love, joy, peace, longsuffering, gentleness, goodness, faith, meekness, temperance.

Today: Pray for joy, strength & happiness.

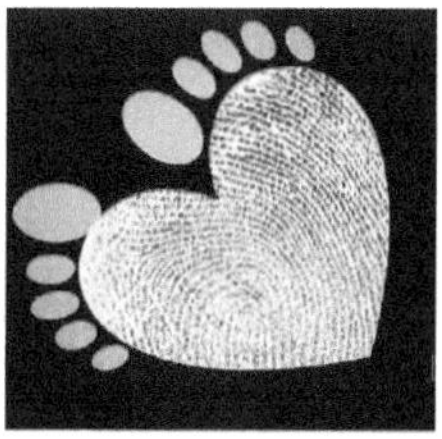

If we ask anything according to His will,

He hears us.

1 John 5:14

TODAY I FEEL…

Your Reflection – Day 14

Complete your journal entry. List all of your emotions, things that are taking place in the NICU, and your prayers.

Date: __/__/____

Today: Pray for life, health & healing.

GIVE IT TO GOD

Yesterday's Entry, Today's Prayer – Day 15

Yesterday you wrote a journal entry. Today, we're going to pray together concerning all the things you listed.

Read this prayer out loud:

Dear Heavenly Father,

First and foremost: Thank you. Thank you for allowing me to see this day. Thank you for the new mercies, grace and favor that you have given me this day. Thank you for keeping me and my family. Thank you for your traveling grace to my home and the NICU every day. Thank you for being my friend and always being here with and for me. Thank you for answering my prayers! Thank you! I don't take you, life and this moment for granted. Before I ask of thing, I just want to say thank you.

Heavenly Father, please forgive me. Forgive me of my sins that I have committed and the sins I didn't realize I have committed. I apologize and ask that you forgive me. Please create in me a clean heart and renew the right spirit within me.

Father, you see everything I have written. I'm giving you all of my cares, anxieties, doubts, fears and stress. From what's currently going on in the NICU to my home and the things that I struggle with privately. I give it all to you. You died for me and all of my issues. In faith, I give you my stress and worries and I believe you will take care of it all. You said in your word to cast all of my anxiety on you because you care for me. I believe your word and I trust you.

Father God, I am doing my absolute best, but I cannot do this without you. I need you not only in my situations but also in my life. In my baby's life, my family's life, in our home and in our hearts. I rebuke Satan and evil spiritual wickedness. No weapon formed against my baby and our home shall prosper. I believe you heal, deliver, and rescue my baby in the NICU as well as our entire family. In Jesus's name I pray, Amen.

If you wish to pray and talk to God more, feel free to do so. Continue to cast all of your cares upon God. He loves you, He cares for you, and He will always and forever be with you.

Get in the habit of giving all of your troubles and cares to God. *If you would like to give your life to Christ, please turn to the* ***Repentance Prayer*** *along with additional prayers.* *(page 124).*

LET'S TAKE A LOOK

Another Form of Reflection – Day 16

In comparison from when you started this devotional, let's take a look at the areas we've discussed and make goals for growth and moving forward.

My Hope (Has my hope increase?):

My Prayer Life (Has my prayer life increase/changed):

My Support System (Is my circle of life positive):

My Faith (Has my faith in prayer increased?):

This exercise is easy, fun and relaxing. Don't over think it. From what you have learned, discovered and gain, make note of it and keep it for key references. **Today: Be grateful.**

REST

Today is 'I Don't Care' day! REST! – Day 17

Genesis 2:2

"By the seventh day God had finished the work He had been doing; so on the seventh day he rested from all his work."

Use this day to rest. In spite of all that needs to be done, in spite of your goals, in spite of your desires to handle certain tasks; use this day to do absolutely nothing. It's a scary thought, isn't it? Sitting on your couch or laying in your bed all day and telling the world "no, not today" it's a crazy thought! But—it's a powerful action. It allows you to mentally, physically, emotionally and spiritually gain strength so you *can* continue your journey. You have to take care of your yourself! If resting is getting your nails done, then do it. If resting is playing golf, then do it. If resting is watching movies on Netflix all day, then do it. Do whatever it is to help you relax and be at peace. You won't be able to continue if you don't take care of you.

Take your trips to the NICU and rest today.

Today: Laugh as much as possible.

PRAYER

Talk to God – Day 18

Matthew 6:9-13

Let us pray:

"Our Father which art in heaven,
Hallowed be thy name.
Thy kingdom come,
Thy will be done in earth, as it is in heaven.
Give us this day our daily bread.
And forgive us our debts, as we forgive our debtors.
And lead us not into temptation,
But deliver us from evil.
For thine is the kingdom, and the power, and the glory, forever.
Amen."

There's no such thing as praying too much. You can talk to God whenever you want. You can tell God whatever is on your heart. Even if you wanted to have a friendly conversation with Him, you can do that. *What does a friendly conversation look and sound like?* I'm glad you asked! I have moments of when I'm by myself and I talk to God as if I'm talking to my best friend. I tell Him how I'm feelings within that moment, what made me laugh, what annoyed me, etc. Why? Because we have that option and freedom to do so! Keep in mind that God is not a genie or a musician. Don't just go to Him in trouble, but go to Him because He's God and He's our friend. Today, get in the habit of randomly talking to God. Tell God "I appreciate you" or "Thanks for being my friend". If something happens and you want to tell Him right in that moment, do it! Example: if someone mistreats you tell God "you know what God; I didn't appreciate that. Please help me to deal with it." And then go on about your business.

I welcome you to do this activity because sometimes, there's no one else that can understand us but God. Sometimes we deal with certain things that takes us away from our own self and we have a hard time dealing with; and don't know what to say or how to handle it. Talking to God help's keep us together. Talking to God help's our sanity.

Make today a wonderful day of great conversations with God!
Today: Make God your friend.

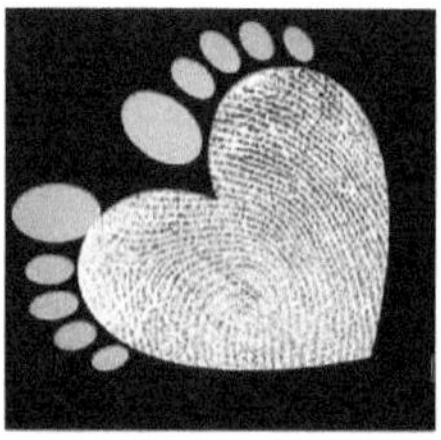

Take delight in the Lord

&

He will give you the desires
of your heart.

Psalm 37:4

ENCOURAGING SCRIPTURES

Scriptures on Prayer – Day 19

1 Thessalonians 5:16-18 Rejoice always, pray continually, give thanks in all circumstances; for this is God's will for you in Christ Jesus.

Philippians 4:6-7 Do not be anxious about anything, but in every situation, by prayer and petition, with thanksgiving, present your requests to God. And the peace of God, which transcends all understanding, will guard your hearts and your minds in Christ Jesus.

Colossians 4:2 Devote yourselves to prayer, being watchful and thankful.

Mark 11:24 Therefore I tell you, whatever you ask for in prayer, believe that you have received it, and it will be yours.

Jeremiah 29:12 Then you will call on me and come and pray to me, and I will listen to you.

Romans 12:12 Be joyful in hope, patient in affliction, faithful in prayer.

Matthew 6:7 And when you pray, do not keep on babbling like pagans, for they think they will be heard because of their many words.

Psalm 145:18 The Lord is near to all who call on him,
to all who call on him in truth.

Jeremiah 33:3 'Call to me and I will answer you and tell you great and unsearchable things you do not know.'

Matthew 6:6 But when you pray, go into your room, close the door and pray to your Father, who is unseen. Then your Father, who sees what is done in secret, will reward you.

Psalm 18:6 In my distress I called to the Lord; I cried to my God for help. From his temple he heard my voice; my cry came before him, into his ears.

James 1:6 But when you ask, you must believe and not doubt, because the one who doubts is like a wave of the sea, blown and tossed by the wind.

Psalm 66:17 I cried out to him with my mouth;
his praise was on my tongue.

John 14:13 And I will do whatever you ask in my name, so that the Father may be glorified in the Son.

1 Chronicles 16:11 Look to the Lord and His strength; seek His face always.

2 Chronicles 7:14 If my people, who are called by my name, will humble themselves and pray and seek my face and turn from their wicked ways, then I will hear from Heaven, and I will forgive their sin and will heal their land.

Job 22:27 You will pray to Him and He will hear you, and you will fulfil your vows.

James 5:13 Is anyone among you in trouble? Let them pray. Is anyone happy? Let them sing songs of praise.

Psalm 17:6 I call on you, my God, for you will answer me; turn your ear to me and hear my prayer.

Psalm 102:17 He will respond to the prayer of the destitute; he will not despise their plea.

Luke 18:1 Then Jesus told His disciples a parable to show them that they should always pray and not give up.

Romans 8:26 In the same way, the Spirit helps us in our weakness. We do not know what we ought to pray for, but the Spirit Himself intercedes for us through wordless groans.

1 Timothy 2:1 I urge, then, first of all, that petitions, prayers intercession and thanksgiving be made for all people.

Today: Pray for a prayerful heart.

TODAY I FEEL...

Your Reflection – Day 20

Complete your journal entry. List all of your emotions, things that are taking place in the NICU, and your prayers.

Date: __/__/____

Today: Pray for progress in the NICU.

GIVE IT TO GOD

Yesterday's Entry, Today's Prayer – Day 21

Yesterday you wrote a journal entry. Today, we're going to pray together concerning all the things you listed.

Read this prayer out loud:

Dear Heavenly Father,

First and foremost: Thank you. Thank you for allowing me to see this day. Thank you for the new mercies, grace and favor that you have given me this day. Thank you for keeping me and my family. Thank you for your traveling grace to my home and the NICU every day. Thank you for being my friend and always being here with and for me. Thank you for answering my prayers! Thank you for progress in the NICU. Thank you! I don't take you, life and this moment for granted. Before I ask of thing, I just want to say thank you.

Heavenly Father, please forgive me. Forgive me of my sins that I have committed and the sins I didn't realize I have committed. I apologize and ask that you forgive me. Please create in me a clean heart and renew the right spirit within me.

Father, you see everything I have written. I'm giving you all of my cares, anxieties, doubts, fears and stress. From what's currently going on in the NICU to my home and the things that I struggle with privately. I give it all to you. You died for me and all of my issues. In faith, I give you my stress and worries and I believe you will take care of it all. You said in your word to cast all of my anxiety on you because you care for me. I believe your word and I trust you. Wither big or small, I give you all of my issues. I ask for strength, peace, joy, healing and victory over my baby's life. One day soon we will be home and this will be all over. And when this is all over, God, I will still need you in my parenthood and life.

Father God, I am doing my absolute best, but I cannot do this without you. I need you not only in my situations but also in my life. In my baby's life, my family's life, in our home and in our hearts. I rebuke Satan and evil spiritual wickedness. No weapon formed against my baby and our home shall prosper. I believe you heal, deliver, and rescue my baby in the NICU as well as our entire family. In Jesus's name I pray, Amen.

If you wish to pray and talk to God more, feel free to do so. Continue to cast all of your cares upon God. He loves you, He cares for you, and He will always and forever be with you.

Get in the habit of giving all of your troubles and cares to God. *If you would like to give your life to Christ, please turn to* ***Repentance Prayer*** *along with additional prayers.* *(page 124).*

I REMEMBER WHEN…

My Reflection, Your Encouragement – Day 22

One morning, I arrived at the NICU early. It wasn't my son's touch time yet and the nurses were all changing shifts. At that point, I had been at the hospital so long, that I developed friendships along the way. With that being said, I used my extra time to make my rounds and say hello. Once I finally got into the NICU, I started my daily routine with my son. In the midst of changing his diaper, one of his nurses came over and said, "Mommy, we need to talk. Can you multi-task? Is it ok if we can talk while you tend to 'Little Man'?" I took a small pause and looked at her in her eyes and said confusingly, "Sure?" She immediately smiled and continued, "Oh no, it's nothing bad! I'm sorry if you took it that way. What I'm about to say is the best news ever!" She walked over to the other side of his bed and gently gave my son her pinky. "Everything is perfect! He's maintain his normal temperature, he's no longer on room air (for quite some time now), he's eating out of the bottle or nursing with every feed, he's awake when it's time to eat, he's picked up two pounds since yesterday and overall maintaining his weight as well. So, with that being said, it's time to start preparing for home! Congratulations!" I wrapped the spoiled diaper up and whispered with excitement, "Yay!"

I finally got settled in my chair and started to nurse my son. I was so overwhelmed with excitement that I wanted to cry so bad but couldn't. Truthfully? I became a little fearful. I had prayed for a long time for the NICU experience to be over and to take my baby home so we could start our lives together; and oh my goodness it was finally happening! When I look back at this moment, I laugh because, I prayed for that moment, God honored my prayer and a new set of fears tried to settled in. I was moving to the next level of motherhood.

When God answer's your prayers, don't allow the devil to rob you of your victory moment. Be excited and ready for the next phase. In fact, start adding to your prayer "Lord, help me to be ready for my baby when he/she comes home." Moving to the final phase of the NICU is a true victory and major triumph! If you're not in route now, pray to be ready for when the baby comes home. Make faith steps and prepare now.

Today's prayer: Pray a new prayer for when baby comes home.

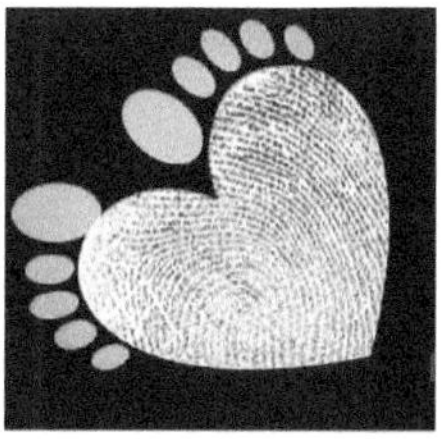

Let us not become weary in doing good;

For at the proper time,

We will reap a harvest if we do not give up.

Galatians 6:9

REST

Today is 'I Don't Care' day! REST! – Day 23

Psalm 4:8

"In peace I will lie down and sleep, for you along, Lord make me dwell in safety."

The closer I got to my son's release date, I took it upon myself to have these types of days more often. I didn't over think anything and made sure I had no stress. I strongly believe days like this (Rest Day) helped me get my mind together with bringing my son home.

As I mentioned before: Use this day to rest. This is a powerful action! It allows you to mentally, physically, emotionally and spiritually gain strength so you *can* continue your journey. You have to take care of your yourself! Pick an activity that helps you and ensures you to relax.

You won't be able to continue if you don't take care of you.

Take your trips to the NICU and rest today.

Today: Smile, eat & sleep.

INSPIRING QUOTES FOR NICU

From Awesome People Around the World – Day 24

"Life is a succession of lessons which must be lived to be understood" ~ Helen Keller

"Cultivate the habit of being grateful for every good thing that comes to you, and give thanks continuously." ~ Ralph Waldo Emerson

"You never know how strong you are, until being strong is your only choice." ~ Bob Marley

"Don't be afraid of your fears. They're not there to scare you. They're there to let you know that something is worth it." ~ C. Joyce Bell

"Having a baby is one of the most wonderful things in life, as well as the hardest thing in your life." ~ Nuno Bettencourt

"There will be many times you feel like you've failed. But in the eyes, heart and mind of your child you are Super Mom." ~ Stephaine Precourt

"Always remember, you are braver than you believe, stronger than you seem and smarter than you think." ~ A.A. Milne

"Challenges are what makes life interesting and overcoming them is what makes life meaningful." ~ Joshua J. Marine

"When you hold your baby in your arms for the first time, and you think of all things you can say and do to influence him, it's a tremendous responsibility. What you do with him can influence not only him, but everyone he meets and not for a day or a month or a year but for a life time. And eternity." ~ Rose Kennedy

"Too often we underestimate the power of a touch, a smile, a kind word, a listening ear, an honest compliment, or the smallest act of caring, all of which have the potential to turn a life around." ~ Leo Buscaqlia

"A baby is born with a need to be loved and never outgrows it." ~ Frank A. Clark

"Be kind, for everyone you meet is fighting a hard battle." ~ Ian Maclaren

"Nothing is impossible. The word itself says I'm Possible!" ~ Audrey Hepburn

"It's amazing the things that you cry at. I cry when I smell my son's hair in the morning. We have a moment of peace and I'll be like, 'Ahhhh! How can you love this much?'" ~ Lena Headey

"In the middle of every difficulty lies opportunity." ~ Albert Einstein

"Most of us, swimming against the tides of trouble the world knows nothing about, need only a bit of praise or encouragement – and we will make the goal." ~ Jerome Fleishman

"It's not the mountain we conquer but ourselves." ~ Edmund Hillary

"Do what you can, with what you have, where you are." ~ Theodore Roosevelt

"I realized this week that I just cannot do it all. So I will choose to do what I can, fabulously." ~ Clinton Kelly

"When life gets too hard to stand, kneel." ~ Anonymous

"You don't always need a plan. Sometimes you just need to breathe, trust, let go and see what happens." ~ Mandy Hale

"We're not built to master it all. Instead we are built to trust God *with all.* So, take each day and each moment, one step at a time." ~ Mariann W. Shaw

Today: Thank God for peace.

TODAY I FEEL…

Your Reflection – Day 25

Complete your journal entry. List all of your emotions, things that are taking place in the NICU, and your prayers.

Date: __/__/____

Today: Give thanks.

GIVE IT TO GOD

Yesterday's Entry, Today's Prayer – Day 26

Yesterday you wrote a journal entry. Today, we're going to pray together concerning all the things you listed.

Read this prayer out loud:

Dear Heavenly Father,

First and foremost: Thank you. Thank you for allowing me to see this day. Thank you for the new mercies, grace and favor that you have given me this day. Thank you for keeping me and my family. Thank you for your traveling grace to my home and the NICU every day. Thank you for being my friend and always being here with and for me. Thank you for answering my prayers! Thank you! I don't take you, life and this moment for granted. Before I ask of thing, I just want to say thank you.

Heavenly Father, please forgive me. Forgive me of my sins that I have committed and the sins I didn't realize I have committed. I apologize and ask that you forgive me. Please create in me a clean heart and renew the right spirit within me.

You know what Father; things are a lot better than before. Sometimes I feel like the absolute worse has happened, but then I am reminded of how far you've brought me, my family and most importantly my baby. I'm taking each moment with one step at a time. I will continue to believe and trust in you for my baby's healing and complete deliverance. I am trusting in you that this journey will come to an end and my baby and I will finally be home together.

Father God, I am doing my absolute best, but I cannot do this without you. I need you not only in my situations but also in my life. In my baby's life, my family's life, in our home and in our hearts. I rebuke Satan and evil spiritual wickedness. No weapon formed against my baby and our home shall prosper. I believe you heal, deliver, and rescue my baby in the NICU as well as our entire family. In Jesus's name I pray, Amen.

If you wish to pray and talk to God more, feel free to do so. Continue to cast all of your cares upon God. He loves you, He cares for you, and He will always and forever be with you.

Get in the habit of giving all of your troubles and cares to God. *If you would like to give your life to Christ, please turn to* ***Repentance Prayer*** *along with additional prayers.* *(page 124).*

No matter how much it hurts now,
Someday you will look back and realize your struggles changed your life for the better."

~ Anonymous

SERENITY

Your Peace – Day 27

Psalm 29:11

"The Lord gives strength to his people; the Lord blesses his people with peace."

Imagine a mother of seven children sitting in the middle of their living room. All seven children are under the age of five. They are running, screaming, playing, crying, banging, throwing, fighting, kicking and laughing. During this moment of chaos, the mother is sitting calmly in the middle of it all with her eyes closed and a smile on her face. She's not yelling back, chasing, screaming or crying herself. She's literally sitting there not moving, breathing calmly and smiling. Impossible? Not necessarily. Look at the overall bigger picture of this scenario and see if you can apply it.

In the midst of your NICU journey, with everything that's going on around you, balancing your home and the hospital, preparing for the baby to come, paying your bills, learning the medical bills, overcoming medical procedures and issues, etc. Within all of it, make it a demand to have peace. Especially within your emotions. You want to scream, cry, snap, go off, fall apart, or just lay on the ground and make everyone else walk the other way. You might want to do all of this, but don't give in to the chaos that's going on around you. It's twirling and spinning completely out of control but you are able to put your foot down and say, "everything may happen all at once, everything may continue to spin like crazy, but through it all, *I will have my peace.* I will have my complete serenity.

Having this level of peace keeps your sanity. You're able to sleep and get rest at night. No matter where you are, your atmosphere at some point is subject to it. I notice now with my toddler, the moment he gets out of control, if I choose to break down, fall apart and yell back, my serenity atmosphere is gone. Meaning: we're both out of control. Standing firm within that moment and saying, "God has given me power to speak those things as though they are and I demand peace within this situation", peace is given. Peace is so important to me, because it out weighs chaos. In moments that you want scream, lose it and fall apart but somehow manage *not to*? That's peace. With everything taking place and to be able to say, "I still have my peace" is a blessing.

Today: Have a moment of silence. Sit still. Inhale. Exhale. Think about your blessings and thank God in your heart. Get in the habit of creating and maintaining peace.

ENCOURAGING SCRIPTURES

Scriptures on Peace – Day 28

Colossians 3:15 Let the peace of Christ rule in your hearts, since as members of one body you were called to peace. And be thankful.

Galatians 5:22 But the fruit of the spirit is love, joy, peace, forbearance, kindness, goodness and faithfulness.

1 Peter 3:11 They must turn from evil and do good; they must seek peace and pursue it.

James 3:18 Peacemakers who sow in peace reap a harvest of righteousness.

Philippians 4:7 And the peace of God, which transcends all understanding, will guard your hearts and your minds in Christ Jesus.

Psalm 34:14 Turn from evil and do good; seek peace and pursue it.

Isaiah 26:3 You will keep in perfect peace those whose minds are steadfast, because they trust in you.

Isaiah 26:12 Lord, you establish peace for us; all that we have accomplished you have done for us.

John 14:27 Peace I leave with you; my peace I give to you. I do not give you as the world gives. Do not let your hearts be troubled and do not be afraid.

2 Thessalonians 3:16 Now may the lord of peace Himself give you peace at all times and in every way. The Lord be with all of you.

Romans 15:13 May the God of hope fill you with all joy and peace as you trust in Him, so that you may overflow with hope by the power of the Holy Spirit.

1 Corinthians 14:33 For God is not a God of disorder but of peace – as in all the congregations of the Lord's people.

Psalm 29:11 The lord gives strength to His people; the Lord blesses His people with Peace.

Psalm 4:8 I will lie down and sleep in peace, for you alone, oh Lord, make me dwell in safety.

Today: Pray for joy, hope, faith & peace.

YOU ARE A BEAUTIFUL PARENT

My Encouraging Words for You – Day 29

1 Thessalonians 5:11

"Therefore encourage one another and build each other up, just as in fact you are doing."

Your way of being introduced into parenthood is a unique way. It's somewhat delayed as to when you can bring you baby home, touch your baby, hold your baby and go into the full swing of parenthood around the clock. The things you have to do to ensure you don't miss a day, moment and opportunity is beyond amazing. Sometimes, life deals us a card that is unfair. It hurts. It's confusing. Even after making lemonade from the lemons it gave you originally, sometimes, it turns the lemonade into bitter/sour water that can't be consumed at all. It's too much.

But you know what? You're doing it! One day at a time, you're getting through it! I believe in my heart that God smiles at the fact that we're moving forward with it. The fact that we even try speaks volumes to Him. We could give up, not do anything and remain in our emotions; but we don't, we move forward. And believe it or not, that's faith! It's faith, hope, its trust and strength. Give yourself credit every single day you get up and strive to the NICU. Because it's not easy and it's not always simple.

Dear Heavenly Father,

I pray a special prayer for the person that's reading this devotional right now. I'm asking that you do a miracles work in their baby and family's life. I am asking that you show yourself strong in their situation(s). Bring forth your complete healing power and simply do what you specialize in: the impossible. Do a complete work of healing, deliverance and restoration in this reader's life. Give them peace, comfort, strength, faith and hope through their neonatal experience. Let them also experience joy. Let the good outweigh the bad, Heavenly Father.

I come against the devil that brings doubt, negative thoughts, disease and illness of any kind. I come against the devil that tries to give the reader backlash for even doing this devotional.

Heavenly Father, let the reader and their family see and experience you in a different lite. I pray that they invite You not only into their NICU journey, but their lives. Let them know you will never leave them or forsake them and that you are always there. God, we thank you for the many blessings that are to come. We thank you for the healing, deliverance, and peace you will provide. And through it all God, we thank you. In Jesus' name we pray, Amen.

TODAY I FEEL…

Your Reflection – Day 30

Complete your journal entry. List all of your emotions, things that are taking place in the NICU, and your prayers.

Date: __/__/____

Today: Give thanks.

REFLECT ON YOUR NICU JOURNEY

Journal Entry

Date: __/__/____

PRAYERS

Healing:

Dear God – Please touch and heal my baby as well as my entire family. Your Son, Jesus Christ was pierced through for our transgressions, crushed for our iniquities; the chastening for our well-being fell upon Him and by His scourging we are healed. I believe and trust in you for complete and total healing. In Jesus' name I pray, Amen.

Repentance & Guidance:

Dear God – Please forgive me of all my sins. Create in me a clean heart and renew the right spirit within me. I admit, I was wrong and I repent right now. I ask that You come into my heart, my life, and my mind. I believe that You sent your Son, Jesus Christ to die on the Cross for my sins. I believe that He rose on the third day, just for me! God, please guide and direct me during our neonatal journey. Give me what to ask and say to the doctors and specialist. In your word, you encourage me to acknowledge you in all my ways and you shall direct my paths. I am trusting in you and your word to help lead and guide me and my family through this journey. In Jesus' name I pray, Amen.

Joy:

Dear God – Some days are harder than others. In moments when it seems like I will never smile again, in moments when it still hurts to smile, in moments when I don't have energy to smile, please help me. Be the lite in my world and in my life and help me to smile and have joy in spite of. You said in your word that weeping only endures for a night but joy comes in the morning. Please be my strength and my joy. In Jesus' name I pray, Amen.

Peace:

Dear God – Please grant me peace during my neonatal journey. Sometimes decisions and outcomes are hard. Sometimes, it seems as though too much is going on for me to truly understand all that's taking place. In your word, you encourage me to keep my mind on you; and if doing so, you will keep me in perfect peace. Please help me to mediate on you. In Jesus' name I pray, Amen.

Strength:

Dear God – Your word says "those who hope in the Lord will renew their strength. All of my hope is in you. I need you and I needs your presence and strength to help get me through this journey. In Jesus's name I pray, Amen.

NICU BUDDY PROGRAM

Our Program's Objective: Is to create a system that works with the neonatal visits and not against it, while removing unnecessary stress.

Key Pointers:

- **Know your NICU Touch Times:** It is important to know the NICU touch-times because your breast pump, eating and sleeping schedule will be set centered around it.
- **Create A Comfortable Breast Pump Schedule:** Setting the pump and touch times together will be helpful. This way during your NICU visit, if you need to pump, you will (or least should) be able to do it at your baby's bedside. In addition, the highlight pf pumping at your baby's bedside encourages great milk flow.
- **Plan & Prep Meals:** Keep in mind that whatever the mommy eats, the baby will eat. Preparing meals with fiber, proteins and good fats will help ensure both mommy and baby is eating properly and healthy. This will avoid fast food restaurants that are high in salt, preservatives and overall improper nutrition.
- **Sleep:** Rest resets everything and gives strength for the next session/visit. Especially the mommy;

her schedule is already interrupted by the pump schedule. Naps during the day will help eliminate stress, anxiety and irritability while promoting awesome breast milk and flow.

- **Questions:** Never be afraid to ask your Doctor and or Specialist questions. There's no such thing as a bad question.

The Neonatal Journey at times is simply exhausting. Our NICU Buddy Program is to help make sure the parent(s) focus on the baby and their health. If we can help take away unnecessary worry and or stress, then we have succeeded.

If you have additional questions and or concerns, please let our CEO know: mariann@masgnicu.org

Meal Ideals

The following meals are healthy, easy to prep, reheat and make great leftovers:

Spaghetti

- Turkey Tacos/ Taco Salad
- Homemade chick noodle soup
- Homemade vegetable soup
- Homemade chicken potpie
- Homemade vegetable pizza (turkey sausage, turkey pepperoni, etc.)
- Baked / grilled chicken salad
- Mixed fruit bowl (kiwi, anything from the berry / melon family, apples, pineapples, papaya, etc.)
- Lasagna
- Enchiladas w/Mexican rice
- Broccoli, chicken, and cheese casserole

- Turkey cheese burgers with baked fries
- Loaded baked potatoes with turkey meatballs, and broccoli
- Grilled cheese sandwiches with soup (soup of any kind)
- Healthy spots: Subway, Chick-Fil- A, Chipotle, Panera Bread,
- Schlotzky's, or Jason's Deli
- Crockpot ideas: turkey sausage, green bean and potato, turkey chili stew, crockpot chicken, crockpot beef, etc.)

Check out Pinterest for great ideas on oven baked and or crockpot healthy ideas.

NOTE: *As three in your circle to fix a dish for the week, giving you the opportunity to choose throughout the week. For breakfast, oatmeal, cold cereal (raisin brand, etc.), scrambled eggs with toast, or a fruit bowl will help with energy in the morning. *Please note these are meal ideas to help with meal preps and rest. If you have questions or concerns with your health, please contact your physician.**

Create Ideas & List Them Here:

NICU Touch Times:

7am___ 8am___ 9am___ 10am___ 11am___

12pm___ 1pm___ 2pm___ 3pm___ 4pm___

5pm___ 6pm___ 7pm___ 8pm___ 9pm___ 10pm____ 11pm____

Mommy's Breast Pump Schedule:

7am___ 8am___ 9am___ 10am___ 11am___

12pm___ 1pm___ 2pm___ 3pm___ 4pm___

5pm___ 6pm___ 7pm___ 8pm___ 9pm___ 10pm____

The following schedule was my schedule during my NICU journey. This schedule is to give you an idea of how to plan everything together. Please keep in mind that this schedule is not mandatory, this was my schedule. This schedule is used for encouraging/example purposes. Reminder: Know your NICU touch times! It is important to know the NICU touch-times because your breast pump, eating, and sleeping schedule will be centered on it.

After collecting your information, you schedule will look like the example listed below, however, with your times added. The breakfast, snack and meal ideas will all be your choice.

(Example of Mariann's NICU Buddy Schedule)

Touch Times – 8am, 11am, 2pm, 5pm, 8pm, 11pm, 2am, 5am, 8am

8am – pump, eat, and shower
11am – NICU visit and pump at bedside
12pm – eat and rest
2pm – pump, snack, and rest
5pm – pump, eat, and rest *(if you would like to visit the NICU, then your choices would be to NICU visit, pump at bedside, and eat.)*
8pm – NICU visit, pump at bedside, and snack. (you can switch with the 5pm for the visit and make this time your last visit for the night.)

11pm – pump and rest
2am – pump and rest or rest and wait until 3am
5am – pump and rest or rest and wait until 6am
8am – start over and repeat

Name:

Date:

City & State:

Contact Number:

Additional Notes per NICU Parent(s):

Your Personalized Break Down:
Touch Times –

8am –
11am –
12pm –
2pm –
5pm –
8pm –
11pm –
2am – pump and rest or rest and wait until 3am
5am – pump and rest or rest and wait until 6am
8am – start over and repeat

If you disagree with the schedule listed and adjustments need to be made, please contact info@masgniuc.org and we will be happy to assist you.

Let's Add Your Buddy!

Request a supporter to be assigned for a specific day. Example: if you have five supporters, each supporter should stick to every Monday, every Tuesday, etc. (with a possible extra day). If you have more than five supporters, create a floater and or a back-up just in case they are not able to assist. If you only have three supporters or less, create your NICU schedule first and work out time frames that will work.

Your circle should be willing to help with the following:

- Meals / meal prep
- NICU Visits
- Purchasing items from the store
- Any reasonable request from the parents

Note: The more people you have, the easier the rotation will be and it puts an ease on your supporters. Example – if you have 10 friends, ask them to commit one week to you; for the next 10 weeks you have one extra help to go to the store, drive you, help around your home, etc.

Mix Match Example:

- Jon (Mon, Wed, Thurs) Will bring dinner all three days.
- Ebony (Tues, Thurs Fri) Will drive me to the hospital.
- Shay (Mon Tues Thurs) Will take me to the store.**Create Ideas & List Them Here:**

Message from the CEO:

I am a proud NICU mommy (single parent) survivor which means I understand first-hand the many trips to the NICU, back at home, with life all in between. Some days were easy sailing while others were hectic and exhausted. I created a schedule and made a goal to stick to it no matter what. Thank God I had both my mother and godmother's support to help take me places (including the NICU), cooked for me, clean and was simply there. It's easy to become somewhat lost in the midst of it all and that's ok. What matters most? Getting back on track and keeping stress away. I truly hope our program has helped you. You're in my prayers and I wish you all the best of luck!

Mariann W. Shaw

MASG
MAISON ALEXANDER SUPPORT GROUP, INC.

Maison Alexander Support Group Inc.

PO BOX 292172

Lewisville, TX 75029

(972) 603-5165

www.masgnicu.org

"We are here to help, serve & inform."

REFLECT ON YOUR NICU JOURNEY

Journal Entry

Date: __/__/____

REFLECT ON YOUR NICU JOURNEY

Journal Entry

Date: __/__/____

REFLECT ON YOUR NICU JOURNEY

Journal Entry

Date: __/__/____

REFLECT ON YOUR NICU JOURNEY

Journal Entry

Date: __/__/____